For You I Must Skylar Parkar

To my loves

past & present

i have deified you in a way that i shouldn't

loved you to a depth that one couldn't

it was beautiful, it was painful, it was everything, thank you

Meet Me By The Lake

New York, New York

Eighteen
in love
what the fuck?

hand holding was ecstasy
inexperienced millennial

madonna whore
virgin
i swear

not that it mattered
you never cared
i was perfect in your eyes

i'd never felt perfect in my entire
fucking little life

boarded that flight
because at sixteen you made me smile
eyes bright with wonder
heart inexperienced with pain

convinced it was you
only you
anything less would turn my beating heart blue

fuck the red lights
it was eros
it was agape
it was pensive
you were pain

i have loved you
in all of the most tumultuous
and beautiful ways
given the chance would i love you again?

yes
always
forever
yes

New York birthed a harlot
our break up birthed a lot
i was only eighteen

what
the
fuck?

Paradise, My Love

You
are
paradise my love

feels like...
i have adored you for a thousand days

in truth
its been like thirty
in truth
i don't think i'm worthy

want the truth?
i'm scared you'll fucking hurt me

i say this
minus the expletives
you say you won't with expletives

Fuck Sleep

No need to dream
when you're laying next to me
the blessing is being awake
and watching you sleep
i kiss your back & neck
soft & gently

i touch you until your body responds
i crave and want nothing but your love
you sweetly wake and bless me
until i've had more than enough

i know what you want without a verbal response
you gently press into me
have i finally woken you up my love?

Say It

Say the word & i am yours
part the legs
i'll take yours

touch me deep
i'll follow the lead

utter those magic words
say how much you need it
say how much you bleed it

say it my love
just once
say those words and...

Soak The Sheets

It had never happened before
twenty four long years of fake moaning
so why the fuck would it finally happen to me?

heaven is a place where our lips meet
it's almost as though i'd never been kissed before

you didn't say relax
i just automatically did
no need to pretend

no need to perform
the odyssey that is your world
granted me the release

i talk too much
talk more when i'm nervous
but you left me without speech

the gentle and passionate kissing
understanding and blessing
the intrinsic delicacies

you turned me into a goddess
and worshipped at my feet
until my cup runneth over
and i blessed your mouth on repeat

19

broken faucet
no way to stop
you lapped it up

you turned my body into a church
you listened to every sermon
turned the tap on and off on repeat

wouldn't stop until...Fuck
i soaked the sheets

Moonlight

Your
eyes
flicker
differently
in the moonlight

the same way my heart
seems to beat differently when you hold me tight

it feels as though
i have craved you my whole life
it feels as though
i could die

you bite your lips as you ease your way in
taking your time
entranced
i watch your body
as you devour mine

a lamb to the slaughter
our first supper
you smile and say i've never tasted so sweet

and i could do this all the time
i could do this all the time
watch your body
as you devour mine

Felt Like

Spent an eternity thinking i knew how i liked it
soft enough to set my soul at ease

rough enough to escape reality
and for a while there
that was all i needed

but you made me want to exist in all of it
felt like god had visited during every covenant

eyes wide shut
or did you open them?

A Million Faces

A million faces
and all i see is you

a million faces
and yet i'll love you till my heart turns blue

Collide

Forever & A Heartbeat

Heaven
is your heartbeat
the sound of it controls mine
you know this
no getting out
i show this

surrounded by flames
the only option is to retreat
i never say it
because it's an unsaid fact
if you were to leave our world
there would be no turning back

i have the door wide open
showed you a path through the flames

despite all of this
your heart remained
calling our world home
promising to never leave

are we forever & a heartbeat?
are we forever in hell?
who's story is this anyway?
i'm the writer out of the two of us
so i guess its mine to tell

Holy Offering

Sweat
pain
beauty
heartache
give me that and then some

i offer my soul to take
i offer my heart to break
i offer
i offer
i offer

Night One

Consumed by desire
and cravings of the flesh
admittedly i wasn't behaving my best way past my worst

our lips met repeatedly
i fell deep almost immediately
you hold me down and press your blessing on me

fucking delightful
i already know where this is gonna go we're so far into it
there's no way home

Hearts Blessing

You're dripping and its beautiful
you're weak
and i need you more

i lap it up
like never before
making circles around your blessing
your moans get weaker
as i go deeper
fuck
you're a keeper

i hate when people say
i've never done this before
knowing their fucking experts

i have done this before
but this is the first time my head & heart were in symbiosis
the first time it felt thrilling
the sheer beauty that is worshiping another freely

not because it is what you're taught to do
but more of what you want to do
never let that power be taken away from you

And I

If you jump
then i'll jump
i'm to weak to take the lead

if you love
then i'll love
i promise to never to leave

Open Blue

I want to be consumed
in the open blue
my water
your water
no clue which is true

we drowned twice
it was heaven
we drowned twice
no fear of hell
no need to say it
i know i'm under your spell

Nectar Of My Love

The
sweetest
drip

you lap it up
as if i offer it sparingly

you lap it up every time
as if i haven't offered you everything

you lap it up every time
as if i haven't already offered all of me

Along Came A Spider

Safe place
warmth
with the ability to leave me breathless

i died in you
renewed with you
made promises that were meant to be kept
made love and Mary wept

leaving was unspeakable
the love just grew deeper

but you know my moods oscillate
you know the demons often come for my soul to take

my mind plays tricks on me sometimes
pulls me down from my happy place

slowly i began to fight an invisible war
self sabotage was a grenade... i got caught

The Gods Birthed Monsters

Raw
lamb to the slaughter
taste
my heart grew fonder

what a waste it would be to walk away
what a waste it would be to leave the match halfway

your heart
my heart
i have no idea which is beating

your heart
my heart
it hurts but the pain is fleeting

release would mean relief
a cowards way out
your heart is encapsulated with mine
my love there is no doubt

A Lick Of Paint

We bought the expensive kind
farrow & ball
figured if we kept going we'd save the wall

the holes came anyway
its fine you said
just needs a lick of paint
you said
fill the hole with some cement
you said
rinse & repeat

but the walls crumbled as soon as they were fixed
the constant rebuilding made my eyes burn

the constant painting made my heart hurt
maybe our love was a season
one very long evening
now it is the guest at a dinner party that just wont leave

the paint couldn't save us
the cement didn't tame us
then she came knocking at my door

And Where Was Your God?

The disconnect came slowly
but the shock to the system was instant
like realising the holy water isn't holy
but at the worst possible moment

just as we were casting out a demon
we sprayed the monster with some liquid and it smiled

grabbed the bottle and drank it
looked back at us wide eyed
now we were left hoping Jesus would save us

he never came
i prayed harder then ever
it was all in vain

Let It Flame

I'm covered in scars
more than i care to admit
the bones have been broken on numerous occasions

i have mastered the art of repairing
placing a pretty veneer over the pain
fashioning up an umbrella in the rain

being loved like this was such a beautiful thing
too beautiful
i didn't know what the fuck to do with it

scared you'd go and i'd finally break
but not if i pushed you first
not if i was the master of my own demise

told myself i'd break my heart ten times over
than have to suffer through you breaking it once

Hold Me

Hold me
like this is the last time
our eyes will meet

hold me
like this is the last time i have your soul to keep

touch me
no
not like that
touch me deep

its beautiful to know
parts of me are buried within your soul
its calming to know
parts of you are buried within mine

And It Rained

I showered you with blessings
as you cursed my name
i showered you with blessings
knowing things wouldn't be the same

Only You

Sometimes it feels like the stars and moon are in cahoots
determined to keep me awake
with visions of you
only you

what did i do to earn such a blessing?
what did i do to deserve such a curse?

for you are long gone
departed from my world in the most raucous of ways
it took months but i accepted that i'd never see your face

the pain weakens during the day
the demons come to hunt once darkness falls
the demons haven't had enough

feeding off the carcass that is our love
haunting me with visions of us speechless

every night
i am left speechless
unsure if i crave your return
or yearn for you to completely depart

Us

A decade may pass
and i may still struggle to say your name
don't think that i do not feel you
don't think that i cannot heal you
don't think such things

silence is how i mourn
silence is how i release
silence is how i pray
that you will come back to me

And Then There Was Madeleine

Her

It all made sense
until she walked in the room
pre-her
it was you
always you
forever you

i was prepared to mourn you for a lifetime
confusing
i apologise

i swear the poetry wasn't all lies
you follow me this deep
and then our story is compromised

but she answered my poetry with poetry
she went through my soul to core of me

she exists in all the rooms
she said she wouldn't consume
and then she consumed

Madeleine

How the fuck
can someone make you feel embarrassed to hold their hand?
her's was soft and gentle
mines rough to the touch

her skin was dark and scarless
mines pigmented with marks
each telling a different story
pain, heartbreak, no glory

she sat at a table with all of my demons
calm collected unafraid to meet them
she sat at a table with all of my demons
calm collected unafraid to meet them

name
occupation
favourite colour

she was very polite
she loved regardless
she knew i was broken
she stayed the night

Her Heart

I was told we never stood a chance
maybe that is why i stood
head held high

with the undying belief
that our beats were unison
and her soul was home to mine

The Siren

Met her by the lake
offered her my soul to take

she was
the prettiest thing
to come out of that water

i don't wanna be fucking moronic
and say i would have drowned with her

but
if she were drowning
then i'd drown too

saving her?
a cowards way out
not when death would mean we'd be together
in this life and the next

she fell
i fell
a mistake?
yes
heaven?
yes

Clean Cuts

I smile
as
you lovingly grip my throat
you ask
do you want more?

is
that a question?
can't
be a question?

not
when you know the answer
not
when my heart races faster

you toy with my cravings
i have yet to be satiated
you know this
no explosions
you know this

has it been hours?
yes
can i taste my own sweat?
yes

blood
sweat
tears
years

i'll
gladly
hand it over

i smile as you lovingly grip my throat
yes
i want more

A Thousand Summers

Being with her
felt like i was experiencing
a thousand summers
all at once

i had to get out of the sunshine
but it just wasn't worth giving up her love

Collide

A time
may come
when the cravings levitate
and make their way to another
but i have yet to see it
have yet to feel it

the definition
of bliss
all in one kiss

your eyes
your smile
your body on mine
simple blessings

the body keeps score
mine forever knocks at your door

Ocean

your eyes
the abyss
a breathlessness occurs
when i stare into it

thoughts
animalistic
touch
hedonistic

i marvel at the ways
your eyes permeate my skin

take my hand
the shallow end no longer amuses me my love
walk me to the ocean

Sweet Blessings

She trembles
at my touch
our eyes
scream lust

we've dreamt of this moment
on numerous occasions
and yet the ecstasy is debilitating

trust me
i whispered
as i slowly unraveled her

trust me
i whispered
as we walked through a field of desire

trust me
i whispered
as i set her soul on fire

trust me
i whispered
as i planted sweet blessings on her neck

trust me i whispered
as she whimpered on my knee
trust me
i whispered
as we bathed in ecstasy

trust me
i whispered
you belong to me

Afflicted

& i could spend the rest of my life
lost in your eyes
what is this affliction?

i would prefer to be free of it
what is this affliction?
my heart doesn't need it

i tell myself this repeatedly
until my soul starts to believe it

but
my heart
my hearts betrays me

pray for the falling
mourn the fallen

i was never able to get back up
pray for the falling
mourn the fallen

what is this affliction?
don't
say
love

Shy About It

When i say i adore you
i mean i love you
and so...

i adore you
i adore you
i adore you

Dream Sequence

I chased her through a field of desire
hearts and minds on fire

did we think once about the bridges we burned?
did we consider the hearts we'd yearn?

professional heartbreakers
running up and down
committing love crimes

she wasn't safe
i never felt home
maybe thats what i liked about her
it was either her or heartbreak
so onward i'd go

The Devil Cares

She told me not to fall
and yet fall i did
she told me i'd end up head first on the floor

i ignored every warning
the bliss that was knowing her
my god it was blinding
and just like that i fell

straight from her heaven
head first into hell

self inflicted agony
can't be mad at the devil
he didn't see the fall coming
can't be mad at the devil
he's more confused than me

Wall Paper

The writings were on the wall
so i chose not to read it
heartbreak came knocking at my door
i chose not see it

i have written our story into my veins
the love is still fresh and circulating
my arteries cannot take such a change
fuck... the remedy turned to poison

she left before we got to the best part
she left whilst still holding my heart

Love Letters To Madeline

I often harken back
to the first time her heart beat danced on my skin
i often harken back
to the moment i let her in

London is crowded with millions of souls...
and yet my heart cannot cease knocking at her door

London is crowded with millions of souls
and yet her hands are the only ones i wish to hold

i cannot get my mind off our first morning
and the way the sun illuminated her skin
i have worshipped the sun every morning since

i curse & bless the day i met her
in equal measure
i curse & bless the day i met her
there's nothing better

Deified

Oscillating between heaven & hell
if i say your name loud enough
will you appear?

you haunt my mind
terrorise my soul
but rarely do i see you
rarely do i feel you

what a cruel exchange
loving another so naturally
serving them pound & flesh
only to survive on less than crumbs

silence my child
this was never love

Eye To The Sky

Where's Lilith?

I prayed for love
two years later
i stopped
clumsy & foolish i mishandled my heart

dropped it & watched it shatter
too many broken pieces to count

pray for love?
what the fuck was i thinking?

i'm kinky as fuck
doubt god approves of my habits
i'd have better luck praying to Lilith

then you turned up
turns out she heard

somehow you came to exist in every corner of my aerator
at a terrifying viscosity

still can't quite work out if your love is heaven or hell
just a fucking mystery to me

My Muse, My Torturer

I
have
made
numerous attempts to rid it from my body

i have released
it
freed
it
and yet it only seems to fly around my room

i open
windows
doors
i've given it numerous means of escape
but yet our love sits perched on my heart

i flinch
i scream
there have been several failed attempts to scare it

unbreakable
unshakeable
fuck

i remember once being able to hold your heart
and the blessing that was watching you hold mine

i'd give anything to watch yours beat so beautifully once more
now our hearts are back in our bodies

both too afraid to take them back out
Mexican stand off
this was never about clout

the brain says move on
but my body
my body remembers

how can i retain so much love
when i hold it alone

how can i love so much
when you are no longer my home

the yearning
the wanting
confusion
the haunting

i will love others
for that i am sure
but i will always love you more

my muse
my love
my torturer

Stateless

Fear is such a confusing feeling
fear will make you destroy the best love you ever had
steal all meaning

now i am speechless
i took holding your beating heart in my hand for granted
now i no longer have access

the pain is so fragmented
i am falling but never touch the...

some days i am ok
other days it is agony

some days i am ok
other days i pray you'll come back to me

have you moved on?
is our love gone?
have you found someone better for you than me?
the demons stay at the foot of my bed and watch my pain with glee

i apologise
but words aren't enough
when you said you loved me deeply
i was scared

when things got tough i'd disappear
i watched as our home burned down whilst holding the fire hose

found a new plot of land
rebuilt with another soul

i thought it was love
it was not
i thought she was it
she was not

i thought i'd move on from you
i was wrong
i've been selfish
i've been dumb

love unrequited is agony
i'll love you forever unrequited
if it meant one day you'd come back to me

Lust Turned To Flames

I stopped with others
i realised if it wasn't you
then it had no meaning

if it wasn't you
then there would be no feeling

if it wasn't you
if it wasn't you
then what?

In Pain We Trust

I knew it would hurt
yet i am surprised it did
covering my hands in dirt
i come with the holiest of offering
my heart is pure
my lungs are gold
please make me whole
the pain was expected and yet it stings
the pain was expected and yet my ears are ringing
the sting was expected and yet my arms are swollen
the sting was expected and yet my heart is broken

I Miss Your Soul

Will i ever feel your heartbeat dance next to mine?
is that such a foreign want?

an unearthly need?
am i a foolish girl?
wanting foolish things?

Symbiosis

I'm still waiting for my heart to release your soul
it hasn't
i'm still waiting for my heart to release your soul
it won't
i'm still waiting on my heart to become whole
it...

Jealousy

Tooth prick to the heart
tooth ache in my head
i stood and watched our love die
not knowing it was just playing dead

fucking deer in the forest
afraid of the kill
fear left it haunted
still it needed the thrill

i have mourned it tirelessly
worshipped at countless alters
if i let go and you let go
will we stop being haunted?

i have a hold
you have one too
i stood and watched our love die
but it was just a fluke

Hi Bubbs

I have written you into a million love stories
i could write you into a million more
and it wouldn't touch the surface of the depth of my love

maybe i can't stop
because loving you is like breathing
and who the fuck wants to suffocate?

maybe i can't stop because not loving you feels like treason
hell is not feeling your touch again

i love you without reason
i love you without giving a fuck
the day i stop loving you Lilith will rejoice
and Beelzebub will be shit out of luck

Eyes Wide Open

She had a bad habit of needing a hand to hold
meeting one queen

handing a king her crown
interchangeable
one love fails
another begins

no in-between
no time for learning or mourning

the beat would go on
and on
and...

the crash into hell was an awakening
the devil had a lot to say
it was either rinse & repeat
or find another fucking way

being loved is beautiful
loving ones self means more
don't ever think anyones heaven sent
just look at Beelzebub

Twin Flame

Bad As A Heartbeat

Millions of chambers
all with their own role
to stop the hole left by others from getting bigger

to stop the hole left by my father from being a trigger
protection
plain and simple
thats all it did
i thought that was all it should do

and then along came you
suddenly i was comfortable with skipping beats
suddenly i was comfortable with breaks and aches
just as long as you came and put me back together again

suddenly the fast beats meant ecstasy and not fear
suddenly the beats were inconsistent at the thought of you not being there

suddenly my heart had a new home
suddenly it wanted nothing more than to beat next to yours

To Know You

Matters
of the heart
are never fair
but loving you
has never been so clear

knowing you has never felt so unfair
i wish everyone was able to feel all that i've felt

all that i've held
does love feel this way for everyone else?
it should

could heartbreak be on the way?
it could
but i'll love until my last breathe
i'll love until there is nothing left

Magic

Your soul touching mine for the very first time
i've never felt something so pure
i've never had anything make me feel so whole

you fulfilled me without knowing
you think you miss me?
i miss you more

you think you want me?
baby i want you more
you think we are magic?
i've never been more sure

Vows

When asked
answer without hesitancy
will you dig deep and sail this ocean with me?

i don't want to belong to you
not when i belong to me

we offer up our love and souls daily
an offering to mother nature
no blessing greater

choosing each other when it makes sense
only if it makes sense
instead of being reckless

i choose to love you
but i am not consumed
by my love for you

devotion is earned
not offered immediately
i cant love you endlessly angel
not when i need to channel some of that love to me

Twin Flame

Blood of my blood
felt like flesh of my flesh
brought back my heart
from the dead

found all the beautiful parts
i'd hidden in fear of the demons

i know i should live for me
and after previous instances
i do
but nothing is more beautiful
than living life with you

Long After

And
i
could
love you for a thousand lifetimes

long after
you leave this earth
long after
our bones have turned to dirt

long after
long after
long after

Love But Make It Healthy – Bad Habits

If we don't last
if fate
swings in the opposite direction &
we fall apart

i hope i get a second chance next lifetime
&
the one after that

i tell myself otherwise
but we both know
i could love you for an eternity

i no longer believe in possession
but you belong to me
without belonging to me

an existence without you?
unbearable
like a life without a cup of tea
yes i would manage
but i'm British
how fucking depressing would that be?

Tell Me The Prettiest Things

Come here my love
tell me the prettiest things

let me stare into your eyes as you tell me you love me
promise to never let a lie spring from those pretty lips

i know you cant promise me forever
that's the silliest thing

Still I Crave

Your eyes pierce through me
in the most beautiful way

when you depart
i find traces of you
for the rest of the day

i recreate every moment
relive every touch
i don't know if i could ever grow bored of your love

Laced

I loved you enough to write a collection of poems

i love you enough to write several more

Let Me Count The Ways

Loving you was an earthquake
my world shattered
and renewed

loved you in different plains
and multitudes
loved you through oceans
sand and calm sea

loved you more than i loved me
damn that was dumb
but true
i'm doing better now
there is a me without you

being loved by you was a drug
i don't do drugs
but fuck
it felt like drugs

sleep no release
dreams?
fleeting
but it is only in my dreams
that we meet once more

given the choice
i'd do all it all again
knowing the outcome
i'd give you my heart to break

it was a blessing falling for you
knowing you
holding your heart
watching it peacefully beat

fuck
you were a difficult lesson
a class i had no interest in taking
through you i learned all the different ways a heart could break
and ache
and...

every now and then
i revisit us
and walk through the ruins of our love

i miss your soul
and
your touch
your lips
your eyes
your body on mine

i know i said "loving you was"
but there is no "was"
i love you infinitely
there isn't enough poetry
to express how much you mean to me

it is you
it will always be you
and for you my love...i must

A Beautiful Exchange

You turned me into art

i turned you into poetry

Thank you to my sisters Sophiea and Ella for supporting me through every stage of my life and this book in particular.

Thank you Tarik, Lauren, Florence and Kellie for always believing me.

Thank you Jackie, for proofreading and generally being the kindest soul on earth.

Thank you Kate Brindley and Belle Place, for your support, guidance and kindness.

Thank you to AJ for consistently working with me and taking beautiful pictures of me.

Thank you Fernanda, thank you for so much, more than I can list, so I'll say thank you for everything.

Cover Photography: A.J Hamilton
Cover Design: Marta Úrbez
Typefaces: ABC Arizona Serif and ABC Gaisyr

First published 2022

© 2022 Skylar Parkar

ISBN 978-1-7396-0250-5

Printed in Belgium